Meet the window box: by far the most accessible garden for any skill level, space, or quality of light. Whether your window faces south where the sun floods in or north with nothing but shade, these indoor and outdoor projects show you how to easily grow succulents, herbs, cacti, monstera, and more. Bright photography and instructions take you from understanding soil and watering needs to personalizing your own box, making this a great primer for anyone who's green to gardening.

how to window box

How to Window Box

small-space plants to grow indoors or out

Chantal Aida Gordon & Ryan Benoit

Clarkson Potter/Publishers
New York

For our families,
who showed us how to grow

Contents

Introduction 8

How to Garden in a Window 12

the **Sand Box** 32

the **Herb Garden** 40

the **Tiny Island** 48

the **Sunny Succulents** 56

the **Ice Box** 64

the **Detox Box** 72

the **Danglers** 80

the **Rain Forest** 88

Customize Your Box 160

Resources 172

Acknowledgments 173

Index 174

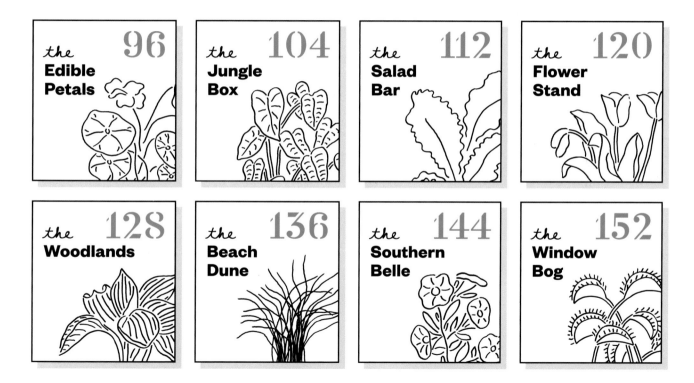

the **Edible Petals** 96

the **Jungle Box** 104

the **Salad Bar** 112

the **Flower Stand** 120

the **Woodlands** 128

the **Beach Dune** 136

the **Southern Belle** 144

the **Window Bog** 152

introduction

A window box can change how you see the world. When you add plants to your line of sight, everything gets greener, brighter, more fragrant, more delicious overnight. Craving leafy greens? Grow and harvest kale and lettuce without leaving the house. Ready to shake off the winter blues come March? Spring tulips and daffodils will cheer you up. Whether you live in a studio or a two-bedroom house, plants can make you happier and more productive. Guided by your light exposure and lifestyle, you'll easily learn how to garden according to your passions in this book.

A window box can be installed on or near the sill of a window, both outdoors and—as we're noticing more than ever—indoors. En masse, window boxes add character to whole city blocks: New Orleans is famed for its impressive bouquets of ferns, sweet alyssum, jasmine, and begonias that blanket upper-floor balconies. In Charleston, South Carolina, tall and spiky "thriller" plants like cordyline are flanked by festive "fillers" like impatiens, while sweet-potato and vinca vine "spillers" fall toward the sidewalk. In Brooklyn, styles are as diverse as the people who live there; on your way to the subway you might catch rows of herbs, stretches of succulents, plots of ranunculus, and, of course, classic ivy crawling up brownstones.

Like most of our friends, we started container gardening while renting; our house in Southern California came with a modest surrounding space that needed attention. Our small garden and our wide-ranging interest in plants challenged us to find inventive ways to grow what we wanted, where we wanted. We began designing our own custom planters when store-bought options didn't match our taste or budget. We wrote about our adventures in gardening on a blog, which we named *The Horticult*, and on it we share our projects and discoveries—from growing philodendron in floating clay pots to learning how to satisfy the hunger of Venus flytraps.

Where to Go from Here

Today, as we embrace smaller and smaller living spaces, there's no better time than now to grow on a more fun-sized scale. In these chapters, we'll show you how to plant, arrange, and care for sixteen window-box gardens. You'll also learn how and where to put your box, depending on the needs of your plants, and how to install it outside and even indoors. Window boxes can also thrive on balcony railings, in front of floor-to-ceiling windows, and along the edges of porches and patios. Are you as design obsessed as we are? See tips throughout for dressing up any store-bought box with paint, grow lights, or trellises.

You can also just use this book as a general care guide for gardening in whatever container you prefer. Ready? Okay, let's start blooming outside the box.

When in Rome

While window-box gardening might seem like a new idea, the trend has been flourishing since ancient Rome. Back then, sills overflowed with medicinal herbs and ornamental flowers so much that the philosopher Pliny the Elder wrote, "Every day the eyes might feast on this copy of a garden, as though it were a work of nature."

How to Garden in a Window

Gardening is not an exact science. It's full of hits, misses, and mysteriously heroic flowers that defy the odds. The great thing about window-box gardening is that you can quickly learn by trial and error from plants you try to grow that end up dying, and from those that thrive. For best results, use our care suggestions here and in the chapters that follow as guidelines; be sure to read any instructions that come with your plant, and, if you'd like, do some extra research. You'll find a robust community online for every genus under the sun; search for your plant plus your concern, and you'll see how other gardeners have made their own darlings prosper. And if a box doesn't do as well as you'd hoped—or doesn't survive the winter—clear it out and start again. That's the freedom of small-space gardening.

Considerations for Outdoor Boxes

The classic window box mounted below a window can vastly improve the curb appeal of your house. Or, for five square feet of green in an apartment or a condo, mount them on metal balcony railings, wood deck railings, and patio plant stands.

- Expect to find a wide range of styles—from simple, decorative, or ornate wood boxes to caged containers made with metal bars and lined with coconut coir. Self-watering boxes are also available.

- Check to see if the window box comes with mounting brackets; if not, you'll need to buy or make your own.

- See if your home's exterior already has a box in good condition. You might still want to paint it to your taste or just to freshen it up. If the existing box is in bad condition, replace it. Check the mounting brackets, which you might be able to reuse. Either way, assess the integrity of your home's facade and its ability to support a fully watered window box (which can weigh over 60 pounds when soaking wet!). When in doubt, hire a handyperson for the installation so you can be sure your mini garden is safe and secure.

- Decide on portability. A smaller box can be moved easily inside during winter months if your plants are not hardy in colder temps. A window box can be moved to a plant stand in a protected area over the winter (see page 94). Also consider color choice when making an exterior/interior box. Painted wood or synthetic boxes will usually last longer in the weather.

- Determine the length and width. Most window boxes line up with the outer edges of the window's trim; measure that span to determine the length of your box.

- Choose the depth. Deeper boxes can insulate plants better and will not dry out or freeze as quickly, but they are often impractically heavy. Be sure that your brackets can support the fully watered weight. Some plants need more soil depth than others, but most will survive and thrive in at least 4 inches of soil.

- Consider your neighbors. If you live in a multistory building, your window box may become a problem for your neighbors downstairs—or for passersby on the sidewalk. Be conscientious of your installation and water when there's no one below. If installed on a balcony rail, your box should hang on the inside of your railing to be on the safe side (and so you can better enjoy the view).

Considerations for Indoor Boxes

While there aren't as many indoor window boxes on the market, you'll find a wide range of styles by searching for rectangular planters, or you can convert an outdoor box. In either case, make sure your container is sealed, has drainage, and includes a water collection tray. See page 162 for details on how to add a liner for indoor use. If you've got a deep sill (7 inches wide or more), indoor window-box gardening is a cinch. Anything smaller, or no sill at all, and you'll need to get a little creative. In this case,

consider installing a shelf below the sill, placing the box on a desk that sits up against the window, or bringing in a stand (see page 94). A plant stand also works great for raising boxes in front of floor-to-ceiling windows.

- Determine the length. If installing on top of your sill, make sure to choose a box that is at least a few inches shorter than the overall length.

- Determine the width. If you're placing your window box on top of a sill, choose a width that doesn't exceed the sill's width. Or make the overhang appear intentional by creating a trellis apron for your box (see page 54).

- Choose the depth. Give your plants (with some exceptions, like succulents and air plants) at least 4 inches of soil depth.

- Hang it up. Not all boxes need a sill or a stand; consider making a hanging window box (see page 85). This is a perfect solution for spilling plants such as hoyas (wax plants), which bloom best in small containers.

- Consider drainage. One of the biggest challenges of indoor window boxes is watering. Be sure your box has adequate drainage holes and a place for the water to go.

Here Comes the Sun

First off, where do you live, and which direction do your windows face? These factors will help you determine the amount of sunlight you'll receive.

The outside shadows of eaves, adjacent buildings or structures, and tree canopies will affect your light levels, so assess any obstructions by checking the spot out at different times during the day. If your area is on the shadier side, we've included boxes for plants that favor less light—like bleeding hearts, monsteras, and sansevierias—which, believe it or not, can be just as fun.

In these chapters, our location recommendations are based on Northern Hemisphere homes. If you're in the Southern Hemisphere, be sure to swap north-facing for south-facing (and vice versa).

If You Want to Geek Out

There are apps for your phone that measure light in foot-candles (fc) through your phone's camera sensor, or you can buy a more accurate meter for about $15. Think of it as a stethoscope for your indoor garden, a valuable diagnostic tool.

When you purchase a plant, you'll usually find a label gives you an idea of how much sun that plant needs. Those recommendations are typically as follows:

For General Outdoor Gardening

FULL SUN Six or more hours of direct sunlight per day

PART SUN Four to six hours of sun per day

PART SHADE Two to four hours of sun per day

SHADE Less than two hours of sun per day

For General Indoor Gardening

BRIGHT/SUNNY Four to six hours of sun directly hitting the window (often in unobstructed south- and west-facing windows, or with a skylight). 1000+ foot-candles

MEDIUM/INDIRECT Four to six hours of incidental sun (often in east-facing windows or obstructed south-facing windows). 250–1000 foot-candles

LOW Less than four hours of sun (often in north-facing windows and heavily obstructed east- and west-facing windows). 50–250 foot-candles

For Window-Box Gardening

"Full sun" outdoors is more intense than "bright/sunny" indoors. Shade-loving plants have more tolerance for direct indoor sun than if placed outdoors. But don't split too many hairs when it comes to sun; window gardening comes down to experimenting with what grows and what doesn't in your space.

Because many of these window-box projects can live indoors or out, we've come up with a simpler sun indicator that you'll find at the beginning of each project.

High	**Full sun** (if outdoors); **Bright/Sunny** (if indoors)
Medium	**Part sun** (if outdoors); **Part shade/Indirect** (if indoors)
Low	**Shade** (if outdoors); **Low** (if indoors)

If you see two recommendations for a box, the first is preferable to the second.

So Which Window Is Best?

Not all sun exposure is the same—it can vary widely depending on which direction the window is facing and even where you live.

South-facing: Your sunniest location fall through spring. During summer in lower latitudes (e.g., Los Angeles and Miami), the sun is too high overhead to project through south-facing windows; relocate sun-loving plants outdoors or under skylights if possible.

West-facing: Warm afternoon sun in summer; four to six hours of sun fall through spring.

East-facing: Gentle morning sun in summer; four to six hours of sun fall through spring.

North-facing: Little to no direct light in winter. You'll get only a few hours of direct morning and afternoon sunlight in summer. Grow low-light plants.

How's the Weather?

Many of the boxes in this book can be grown indoors next to a properly oriented window. And they can all be grown outdoors under the right conditions.

Although it's not definitive, your USDA zone is a good indicator of whether or not your plant can survive outside in your location come winter, otherwise known as hardiness. You will find zones noted in your plant research often on the plant's nursery tag. If you live in the United States, you can look up your USDA Plant Hardiness Zone online by plugging in your zip code.

Your plants' survival outdoors depends on other factors beyond your control—like seasonal precipitation, humidity, and wind. But rather than limitations, think of these as challenges to tackle by, for example, staking your tall foxgloves to withstand wind.

Signs of Sun Deprivation

- Stunted growth

- Loss of leaf color

- Spindly, "leggy" growth

- Longer spaces between leaves

- Failure to bloom

Remember, water and fertilizer are not substitutes for sun—adding more will only hasten a plant's demise. If your plants need a boost, try installing grow lights (see page 166).

Tools

You don't need much to garden in a small space. Plus, any provisions are easy to find. A small hand trowel for digging and scooping soil is essential. Other items helpful to have include a plastic tote for mixing and storing soil, a plastic sheet or trash bag (to minimize mess indoors), a mister or spray bottle, gloves for prickly plants, pruning shears, and a watering can (choose one that you'll want to show off!). If heading outside, don't forget your sunblock and a hat!

How to Buy Plants

You'll find a wonderful variety of specimens at independent nurseries, big-box garden centers, and home improvement stores alike. If you have a plant in mind that's not in stock, nurseries are often happy to order a requested species, or to suggest a place where you can find it. While shopping for plants, select the healthiest ones. Say yes to perky, vibrant leaves and sturdy stems, and, if you're craving flowers, a decent number of buds (so you'll enjoy blooms well into the future). Plants in respectable nurseries are grown in their most ideal temperature and sunlight conditions, so don't despair if your plants go through some shock when you transplant them. Chances are, they'll adjust! Don't take home plants that look mildewy, weak, or as if bugs have nibbled on them. If your pot feels lighter than expected (or if roots are trying to escape from the drain holes at the bottom), this plant might be severely root-bound—a sign that there's more drama on the horizon. Trust us, you don't want those problems. Don't be afraid to take a peek by gingerly tipping the plant out of its container to check for tightly wound roots.

Go ahead and shop online also, particularly for specialty plants like carnivores, rare tropicals, and succulents. Many nurseries will ship plants, bare roots, and seeds to your doorstep or to a local nursery—sometimes for free! You might also hear about people sharing plant cuttings and seeds on social media.

Or check out gardening clubs in your town that might be dedicated to your favorite category of plants or your local botanic garden. You may find meetings and talks by experts or shows and sales where you can buy rare beauties for a song. Check out the resources on page 172 for some names and places.

The Circle of (Plant) Life

Not all plants grow forever, and that's okay. Here's a breakdown of the differences between those that come back and those that need replanting season after season:

Annual: A plant that completes its life cycle (growing from seed, sprouting, flowering, seeding, and dying) in one year. It will probably need to be replaced, although it might self-seed a new generation in a nearby spot; under the right conditions, those seeds might actually germinate! One advantage of annuals? They tend to stay in bloom for a long time. Keep them flowering with a vengeance by pinching off spent blooms before they develop seedpods. An annual has one mission: to have babies! So it will keep pushing out blooms until it seeds. *Examples: borage, nasturtiums, and most marigolds.*

Perennial: A plant that lives for three or more growing seasons, returning year after year, usually blooming for a shorter

---

A Quick Note on Names

In this book we use common names for plants along with their italicized Latin names, which consist of the genus first (always capitalized), followed by the species (in lowercase). Occasionally there's a hybrid or cultivar (a cultivated variety) in single quotes. For example, the paddle plant's Latin name is *Kalanchoe thyrsiflora*. And one type of sansevieria's Latin name is *Sansevieria trifasciata* and its hybrid name is 'Golden Hahnii'. If this information reminds you of Latin class in the very worst way, then just reference the photos throughout this book.

---

amount of time than annuals. Depending on your climate, some perennials, like tulips, are best (and often) grown as annuals, meaning you'll have to replant them every year. *Examples: daffodils, roses, and irises.*

Biennial: A plant that completes its life cycle in two years. After forming its roots, stems, and leaves in the first year, the plant will flower in the second, then reseed and die. *Examples: foxgloves, Queen Anne's lace, and evening primrose.*

Medium and more

You'll need enough soil to fill almost all of your box, minus the plants of course. For a 32" × 7" × 7" indoor box or a 42" × 7" × 7" outdoor box, we recommend starting with a 1.5 cubic-foot bag of potting soil and smaller bags of amendments.

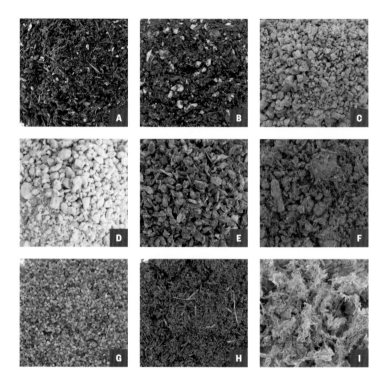

A. POTTING SOIL
A good base for all-purpose potting

B. CACTUS/SUCCULENT SOIL MIX
Supreme drainage powers make this mix excellent for, duh, cacti and succulents

C. PUMICE
Improves drainage, retains water and minerals, aerates soil

D. PERLITE
Improves drainage, retains water, and aerates soil

E. ORCHID BARK, MEDIUM AND SMALL SIZE
Improves drainage, adds organic matter to provide nutrients, can also be used as topping

F. COMPOST
Adds richness and organic matter; mix with soil or add as top dressing; can be stinky!

G. HORTICULTURAL SAND
Improves drainage

H. SPHAGNUM PEAT MOSS OR ALTERNATIVE*
Retains and releases water evenly

I. LONG-FIBER SPHAGNUM MOSS
Absorbs water like a sponge while creating an oxygen-rich environment for carnivorous bog gardens

* Sphagnum peat moss has become a controversial gardening amendment because it's mined from peat bog wetlands that are *verrry* slow to regenerate. (Peat is also extremely difficult to rehydrate once it's dried out.) An alternative includes coconut coir, which helps with water retention.

Surface style

In addition to soil, you want some top dressing for good looks. You can also use a two-in-one medium that serves both form and function; a mulch of orchid bark can both insulate the soil and create a clean look. In many of these boxes, we use these top layers:

A. CEDAR MULCH
Adds nutrients, discourages bugs, good for woodsy themes

B. CLAY PEBBLES
Aid drainage and aeration, cover soil with a terra-cotta vibe

C. COARSE SAND
Helps with drainage, excellent for a desert feel

D. POLISHED JADE PEBBLES
Lend a luxurious, subtle green glow

E. LAVA ROCK
Prevents surface hardening; creates an organic, tropical look

F. SMALL ORCHID BARK
Improves drainage, adds organic matter to provide nutrients, looks pretty

G. POLISHED PEBBLES
Create a smooth, modern surface that goes well with succulents

H. JADE BEAN PEBBLES
Add texture and contrast with larger jade stones; also great on their own

I. MEDIUM ORCHID BARK
Delivers a rugged, woodsy look

Soil Basics

Not only does soil provide the physical support that allows roots to anchor themselves, it also helps your plant take in vital nutrients and regulate water intake. Also important: Plants absorb oxygen through their roots from little air pockets in the soil.

Different plants thrive in different types of soil, thanks to variations in texture, nutrients, and pH. That's why gardeners often create soil mixes tailored to their plants. For example, they might add compost to enrich sandy soil and pumice to improve its drainage. Ten different experts will have ten different formulas for a soil mix for the same plant, so don't be intimidated by our recommended soil mixes (which we try to keep simple anyway). Proportions are approximate; feel free to eyeball, use handfuls, and modify according to what you have available. Here's another helpful tip: When you're unpotting your plants from a reputable source, pay attention to the soil mix that came with the plant. And if all else fails, ask your nursery for recommendations or substitutions.

Discover Your Roots

The size of your box will affect what you can grow; some root systems need to roam far and wide, and they require a large container for their Hulk-like habits. Other plants with deep root systems, like some herbs, can survive in a narrow box as long as the container is tall enough. And then there are the shallow root systems—as seen in succulents, for example—that let you place plants close together and in containers just a few inches deep. (Check out the Tiny Island on page 48, the Sunny Succulents box on page 56, and the Detox Box on page 72 for some beautiful possibilities.)

It's important to loosen the root balls before you plant them. Relaxed roots help a plant anchor itself and find the nutrients it needs once it's in the box (or ground). When you're ready to plant, tilt the provided container (usually plastic) while massaging the sides and bottoms to separate it from the roots. For stubborn root-bound plants that don't want to leave their containers, you may want to cut away the plastic with scissors or garden shears. (You may want to check if the plants are root-bound at the nursery prior to bringing them home. If a plant is too root-bound, it may not be able to recover, even in a larger window box.) If you're transplanting the plant from a clay or ceramic pot, slide a small hand trowel around the inside perimeter of the pot to separate and loosen the soil.

When your plant is free, gently tease the roots from their molded shape. It's okay if a few roots break! But if the root ball is so tight that it's not loosening up with your root massage, soak the root ball for a couple hours until the roots unstick.

Hello, Hydration

Thanks to its raised position, the soil in containers dries out faster than its grounded counterpart. So keep an eye on your garden during the week! The smaller the window box and/or the more hours of sun it gets, the more frequently you'll need to water it.

Keep in mind that overwatering with poor drainage—and not underwatering—is most often the cause of failing flora. Most plants in general rely on soil and containers with good drainage to help prevent their roots from becoming waterlogged, which leads to suffocation and root rot.

So, when is it time to water? Some plants will tell you with sagging leaves or slouching flowers. You can usually tell by sticking a finger into the soil about an inch deep. If the soil feels dry, apply water with a narrow spout directly to the soil and avoiding the leaves so the water doesn't spill out helterskelter onto your rug. Water until the top layer of soil is evenly hydrated and water is visibly running from all drain holes below. For more drought-tolerant plants like cacti, and especially during the winter, you might need to wait for a deeper level of the soil to be dry, while plants like vegetables and woodland flora will need to be watered more often to maintain constant moisture. Topping your soil with mulch or pebbles will also prevent the sun from quickly crusting the top layer of soil.

Raise indoor boxes with blocks of wood to allow room for water collection trays. Use shallow food storage containers or

even tall plastic petri dishes to catch runoff. Every two to three months, pick up the whole box; take it to the sink, bathtub, or outside; and give it a thorough soaking until water flows from the drain holes. Leave it for thirty minutes, then use a water collection tray to catch last drips when you return your box to its perch.

Some plants enjoy misting in addition to watering. This is especially true for air plants (see page 53); you can douse them using a spray bottle a few times a week, or dunk them once every week or two. Oh, and be sure to keep your box away from the heater, or else use a humidifier in the room.

Fertilizing

Plants also need their vitamins. Gardeners usually nourish their plants with fertilizer, which comes in a wide range of forms, formulations, strengths, and sources. There are liquid fertilizers, granular fertilizers, fertilizer from blood meal, and fertilizer from kelp. And that's just scratching the surface.

Pick some up, and you'll likely see three numbers on the front—for example, 5-10-10 or 20-20-20. Each number stands for the amount of three nutrients—nitrogen (N), phosphorus (P), and potassium (K), respectively—contained in the fertilizer. For example, a 5-10-10 fertilizer contains half as much nitrogen as it does phosphorus and potassium. Gardeners abbreviate this trio as NPK, and they like to think of the combination as "shoots, roots, and fruits": nitrogen supports vegetative and leaf growth, phosphorus supports root and flower development, and potassium (or potash) helps the plant develop fruits while fighting stresses like disease.

Plants have their specific needs, but many will benefit from a balanced fertilizer (meaning the numbers are equal) mixed according to the label and applied during the plant's growing season.

Controlled-release fertilizers in granules provide a slow, steady nutrient supply when mixed into the first inch or two below the soil surface. We also like water-soluble fertilizers, which can be diluted easily and mixed directly into your watering can. For outdoor gardening, where sustainability is a concern, organic water-soluble fertilizer won't pollute local streams with the kind of chemical runoff caused by synthetic fertilizers.

Follow these tips for general feeding:

- Wait until at least a month after planting your window box before fertilizing. Potting mixes come preloaded with soil nutrients.

- Don't feed a plant that is not actively growing (such as during the winter). When leaves and stems begin to grow, then add fertilizer.

- Never fertilize dry soil. First give the window box a good watering, then apply enough water-soluble fertilizer until it runs out of the drain holes.

Pruning

A groomed garden is a healthy garden. Even when a leaf or flower is dried out, the plant is still devoting energy to it—resources that are better used in the younger parts of the plant. When your blooms are faded (also known as "spent") pinch off or deadhead that flower with either your fingers or a pair of garden shears. Snip the stem under the flower and right above the first set of healthy leaves. Also, be sure to cut off dying leaves (with some exceptions, like elkhorn or staghorn ferns; see page 93 for details) to redirect the plant's energy to the thriving parts that need to grow.

Pruning also lets you influence the shape of your plants. If you have a lot of greenery in a small box, pruning can help control foliage that threatens to overtake the box and muscle out other plants. Be careful not to prune too much at once; overzealous snipping can cause an imbalance between foliage and roots, leading to panicked sprouting that can exhaust your plant. The best time to prune for shape is at the beginning of a plant's growing season.

> **TIP** Don't spread the infection. After using shears and other tools on a sick plant make sure to clean them well with a water/bleach solution, rubbing alcohol, or hydrogen peroxide.

Replacing

If a plant overgrows the box—or it's gone to the great garden in the sky—feel free to swap it out for a new and possibly different plant that might do better in your window's microclimate. Expect to replace annuals and plants that aren't winter hardy and can't be brought inside.

Pests & Other Problems

The onslaught of tiny critters can destroy a beloved plant within days. Fortunately, a window box is often small enough to let you manually hunt down the culprits and remove them by hand. A blast of cold water from a spray bottle can also wash them away. Neem oil is widely used in organic gardens to disrupt pests. Or you can make an all-natural repellent by mixing water with a few drops of clove essential oil or ground cloves.

Powdery mildew is a common fungal infection that causes an icky white powder to form all over your plants' leaves. Cut off and dispose of the affected foliage and try relocating your box to a sunnier spot.

More Evergreen Advice

—

It's always better to underfertilize than to overfertilize. Signs you may have overfertilized include burnt edges of leaves, drooping lower leaves, blackened roots, and whitened soil surface.

If you tend to forget to water, buy a self-watering box that recycles the drained water. Or get a charming watering can in your favorite color. The more stylish the can, the more likely you are to use it!

Diatomaceous earth (D.E.) is a chalky, naturally occurring powder widely available online and at hardware stores. It can provide effective pest control when sprinkled on and around plants, or amended in the soil. Even better, food-grade D.E. is super easy to find!

Many plants, including irises, English ivy, and tarragon, are toxic. To help protect your pets, check your desired plants against the ASPCA's "Poisonous Plants" online database.

Some people suggest adding a deep layer of rocks to the bottom of a box to help wick away water in boxes that don't have drainage. But there is no way to know the water level and the roots can suffocate or rot as a result. If you want to skip Lining Your Box (see page 162), an alternative method would be cache potting: keeping plants in their original plastic containers and placing them in a decorative box. (We suggest this for the devil's ivy on page 108.) Doing so allows you to take the plant out of the box to water it.

The Boxes

the
Sand Box

Cultivate your very own collection of cacti and euphorbias, spiny sweethearts that flourish in arid, sunny conditions. Nearly all members of the Cactaceae family are succulent, meaning they store water in their foliage and stems. Despite their barbs, these plants can produce show-stopping flowers—or even downright dainty ones. Some resemble daisies or hot-pink horns, and others are in a world of their own: night-blooming, moth-attracting, and the size of baseballs. Wear thick gloves when handling; their spikes range from fiberglass thin to the thickness of sewing needles.

LOCATION
Indoors*

LIGHT
High to medium

WINDOW
South-, west-, or unobstructed east-facing

EASE
Easy

SOIL
Two parts cactus/succulent mix, one part pumice

TOPPING
Coarse washed silica sand

WATER
Low

FEED
5-10-10 liquid fertilizer once in spring, summer, and early fall

* This box can also be grown outdoors. Be sure to check your lowest winter temps against your plants' hardiness. Surprisingly, some species of opuntia can survive in climates as cold as USDA zone 2! For the most part, though, these plants can survive winter only in zone 9b and warmer.

A. *Espostoa lanata*

B. *Cleistocactus* spp.

C. *Notocactus* spp.

D. *Opuntia* spp.

E. *Ferocactus gracilis* subsp.
   coloratus 'El Tomotil'

F. *Euphorbia stellata*

G. *Tephrocactus articulatus*
   var. *papyracanthus*

H. *Mammillaria carmenae* var.
   rubriflora

I. *Echinocactus grusonii*
   (golden barrel cactus)

J. *Echinopsis* 'Dominos'

PLANTER BEWARE While euphorbias may not have the most painful spikes, if jostled or brushed up against, they can "bleed" a milky latex that can be irritating, even toxic, to humans and pets. Handle with caution. Keep the Sand Box out of reach of animals, children, and clumsy adults.

1. Make sure your box has good drainage. If not, drill drain holes along the bottom of the box. Insert a screen cut to the size of the box's bottom to prevent soil from escaping or clogging the holes.

2. Mix the soil and add it in an even layer until your box is two-thirds full. Remove the cacti and euphorbias from their containers using thick gloves.

3. Pour in the soil mix until the box is two-thirds full. Handling the plants by their bases, stage and place them in your desired arrangement. Young cacti and euphorbias have shallow root systems, so place your plants as close as you'd like, keeping in mind that cacti and euphorbias can take on some unexpected shapes. For this box we wildly varied their spacing from ½ inch to 5 inches to create an empty desert look.

4. Fill in the box with additional soil until the entire surface is level, and the bases of the plants are about 1 inch below the top of the planter.

5. Finish the arrangement by top-dressing with up to a ½-inch layer of washed sand.

Create a happy home for your desert-dwelling beauties

Place this box in the sunniest part of your home, a location (indoors or out) that receives four to six hours of direct sun daily. Note that young cacti prefer less sun and more water than their parents.

Water when the first inch or two of soil is dry to the touch. We normally water our cacti about once every four to six weeks in the spring and summer and about once every other month in the winter. Remember: The less light your plants receive, the less water they will need.

Give your plants two months to establish themselves before feeding. Cacti can survive without fertilizer, too; it's always better to underfertilize than to overfertilize.

Remove spent blooms with tweezers. Carefully repot any plants that get too big for the box.

plant with personality

- Insert some dry humor by adding *Mad Max*–inspired accessories—gears, springs, and other shiny bits and bobs. Get them new at (of course) your local hardware store, or find quirkier, more specialized pieces at an industrial surplus shop or online.

- As your plants take shape while they're young, feel free to adjust their positions in the box as you see fit.

the
Herb Garden

A handful of chives will add attitude to your eggs, and some muddled sage can kick up your cocktails. A sniff of peppermint clears the head. But what is an herb exactly? By its most common definition, an herb is a plant used for medicine, fragrance, flavor, or dye. (In stricter botanical terms, the word *herb* means any seed-bearing, nonwoody plant whose stems die back after flowering.) Equipped with some popular herb species, a grow light, and a chalkboard surface for whimsical menus, this box could be your key to more flavorful meals, better moods, and an aromatic home.

---

* This box can also be grown outdoors. Consider timed irrigation, as cilantro and parsley can get thirsty. And of course, skip the grow lights. If you're placing on a sunny side of the house, include light lovers like rosemary. As always, be sure to check your lowest winter temps against your plants' hardiness. Most of these herbs should be hardy in USDA zones 4–10.

LOCATION
Indoors*

LIGHT
Medium

WINDOW
South- or west-facing (if east- or north-facing or obstructed, add grow lights; see page 166)

EASE
Intermediate

SOIL
Two parts potting soil, two parts pumice, one part compost

TOPPING
Clay pebbles

WATER
Moderate

FEED
5-10-5 fertilizer about once a month during spring growing season

A. *Origanum vulgare* (oregano)

B. *Thymus × citriodorus* 'Variegata' (lemon thyme)

C. *Salvia officinalis* (sage)

D. *Coriandrum sativum* (cilantro)

E. *Allium schoenoprasum* (chives)

F. *Artemisia dracunculus var. sativa* (French tarragon)

G. *Petroselinum crispum* (parsley)

1. Make sure your box has good drainage. If not, drill drain holes along the bottom of the box. Insert a screen cut to the size of the box's bottom to prevent soil from escaping or clogging the holes.

2. Mix the soil and add a healthy 3- to 4-inch layer to the bottom of the box.

3. Remove the plants from their containers and loosen the soil around the roots, breaking up any root-bound bundles. Arrange the plants on top of the soil about 4 inches apart.

4. Fill in the box with additional soil until the entire surface is level, and the bases of the plants are about 1 inch below the top of the planter. Feel free to gently adjust the plants until their bases line up across a smooth soil bed.

5. Top-dress the soil with clay pebbles to help prevent the surface below from hardening.

TIP If your cilantro flowers or "bolts," think twice before snipping the leaves for use. Once it bolts, the leaves of this annual will become unsightly and lose their flavor. You can try germinating or drying the seeds, which are known as coriander—spice-rack gold.

Ensure your herbs stay in mint condition

Place the box in a sunny south- or west-facing window, and skip the grow lights. Planting on an east- or north-facing sill? Then you'll likely need grow lights to keep your herbs healthy.

Water before or as soon as the soil feels dry. Some herbs, like sage and thyme, are more drought tolerant; in fact, drier conditions can make your sage even more flavorful. If you'd like, you can use a divider (see page 100) to separate the soil inside your box so you can better control moisture levels, or just water thirstier plants (like cilantro and parsley) directly and more often than more drought-tolerant ones.

To prevent an invasion of caterpillars or aphids, spray your arrangement with neem oil (see page 27).

plant with personality

- Host a dinner party and create a box-to-table dining experience. Paint the outside of your box with blackboard paint and label your plants. Include the herbs in the meal you cook. Then use the box as a temporary centerpiece. Provide culinary scissors so your guests can snip off some extra seasoning for their plates.

- For best results in low light, add grow lights. See page 166 for instructions.

the Tiny Island

Primarily native to tropical regions—the Hawaiian Islands in particular—bromeliads add flash to areas deprived of direct sunlight. The Bromeliaceae family is wildly diverse, encompassing the pineapple plant, Spanish moss, and the ever-popular air plant. Most bromeliads are "monocarpic," meaning a plant flowers only once before dying. But take heart: it's not unusual for a bromeliad's flower to last three to six months. A bromeliad will produce pups, which are mini offshoots that can be gently separated from the waning parent and grown on their own. Online resources like Bromeliads.info provide invaluable guidance on caring for your "bros."

---

*This box can also be grown outdoors. Avoid placing in harsh, direct sunlight; a bright spot under a tree canopy is ideal in USDA zones 10–12. Don't expose to temps below 55°F.

LOCATION
Indoors*

LIGHT
Medium

WINDOW
East- or west-facing, or south-facing with filtered light

EASE
Easy

SOIL
Two parts potting soil, one part pumice, one part fine orchid bark

TOPPING
Black lava rock

WATER
Moderate

FEED
16-16-16 liquid fertilizer diluted to one-half strength

TERRESTRIAL BROMELIADS

A. *Guzmania lingulata* (scarlet star)

B. *Guzmania conifera* (cone-headed guzmania)

C. *Neoregelia carolinae* (blushing bromeliad)

D. *Neoregelia* 'Sheba'

E. *Vriesea splendens* 'Splenriet' (flaming sword)

AIR PLANTS (AKA TILLANDSIAS)

F. *Tillandsia funckiana*

G. *Tillandsia xerographica*

H. *Tillandsia ionantha* hybrid

I. *Tillandsia stricta*

J. *Tillandsia brachycaulos* × *T. schiedeana*

K. *Tillandsia tenuifolia*

L. *Tillandsia juncea*

M. *Tillandsia tectorum*

N. *Tillandsia tricolor* var. *melanocrater* 'Red'

O. *Tillandsia capitata* var. *domingensis*

P. *Tillandsia ionantha* 'Fuego'

1. Make sure your box has good drainage. If not, drill drain holes along the bottom of the box. Insert a screen cut to the size of the box's bottom to prevent soil from escaping or clogging the holes.

2. Mix the soil and add a healthy 3- to 4-inch layer to the bottom of the box.

3. Remove the plants from their containers and loosen the soil around the roots, breaking up any root-bound bundles. Arrange the plants on top of the soil. These plants have small root systems, so they can be spaced very close together.

4. Fill in the box with additional soil until the entire surface is level, and the bases of the plants are about 1 inch below the top of the planter. Feel free to gently adjust the plants until their bases line up across a smooth soil bed.

5. Top-dress the soil with lava rock.

TIP Place air plants on a higher nook or trellis for good air circulation. (See the trellis DIY on page 164.) You know those glass orbs that have become trendy homes for tillandsias? Don't use them. They block airflow and are basically death-bubbles for air plants.

Be nice to your bros

Place your box in a setting with bright, indirect light, like an east-facing window. Some direct sunlight in the morning is okay, as it is gentler than afternoon sun. Feel free to close the blinds a bit if your box is receiving too much direct sun.

Water your terrestrial bromeliads when the first 2 inches or so of soil are dry.

Mist your air plants with a spray bottle twice a week and give them a good drenching under tap water every other week. Shake off any excess water and place them in a spot with good airflow. If plants become dry or hardened, soak the parched plant for up to five hours, keeping any flowers above the water's surface.

For terrestrial bromeliads, feed once a month, applying fertilizer directly to the soil and making sure not to get any in the plants' central "tanks"; for air plants, every other watering, add a small amount of water-soluble fertilizer to your spray bottle. Think 1 teaspoon per gallon.

plant with personality

- A top dressing of black lava rock is a nod to the plants'
  volcanic Hawaiian homeland.

- Add a trellis for your air plants, which will love the air
  circulation. A second apron trellis below your box provides a
  place for your spray bottle and pruners. See page 164.

the
Sunny Succulents

Thanks to their shallow root systems, succulents are a great match for small spaces—you can grow your plants close together without having to worry about unhealthy crowding. There's also an incredible spectrum of textures for you to play with, from the velvet touch of the panda plant to the clustered jelly beans of the stonecrop. Embrace the variety! If your sunlight is scarce, check out sansevierias (page 72) or hoyas (page 80).

LOCATION
Indoors*

LIGHT
High, medium

WINDOW
West- or south-facing

EASE
Easy

SOIL
Two parts cactus mix, one part pumice

TOPPING
Polished pebbles

WATER
Approximately every 3 to 6 weeks

FEED
10-10-10 liquid fertilizer diluted to one-fourth strength every month during spring, summer, and fall

* This box can also be grown outdoors. Give your box fresh air after the last threat of a freeze, or grow year-round in USDA zone 9 and warmer. The succulents will appreciate the extra light and you'll likely get some blooms and blushing foliage.

A. *Portulacaria afra*
(elephant food)

B. *Rosularia chrysantha*

C. *Graptoveria* 'Opalina'

D. *Crassula perforata*
(baby necklace)

E. *Sedum rubrotinctum*
(jelly bean plant)

F. *Kalanchoe thyrsiflora*
(paddle plant)

G. *Aloe* 'Black Beauty'

H. *Echeveria* 'Tippy'

I. *Anacampseros*
telephiastrum variegata
'Sunrise'

J. *Kalanchoe tomentosa*
(panda plant)

K. *Sedum morganianum*
(burro's tail)

L. *Sedum pachyphyllum*
(stonecrop)

M. *Sedum nussbaumerianum*
(coppertone stonecrop)

1. Make sure your box has good drainage. If not, drill drain holes along the bottom of the box. Insert a screen cut to the size of the box's bottom to prevent soil from escaping or clogging the holes.

2. Mix the soil and add a healthy 3- to 4-inch layer to the bottom of the box. If your box is more shallow, just be sure your soil depth is at least 2½ inches—the bare minimum.

3. Remove the plants from their containers and loosen the soil around the roots, breaking up any root-bound bundles. Arrange the plants on top of the soil.

4. Fill in the box with additional soil until the entire surface is level, and the base of the plants are about 1 inch below the top of the planter. Feel free to gently adjust plants until their bases line up across a smooth soil bed.

5. Top-dress the soil with polished pebbles for a smooth, modern feel.

THE GIFT THAT KEEPS ON GIVING Many succulents propagate by cuttings—meaning you can break off a leaf or cut a stem just above the next leaf or set of leaves (using sharp scissors, a knife, pruning shears, or your hands), let it callus for a few days in part shade until you see new roots start to form, and plant it in a new location. Or give cuttings to friends to plant in their own window boxes.

Be sweet to your succulents

Steer clear of low-light and water-heavy situations—both surefire ways to kill your succulents. When you notice the first inch of soil has dried, wait a week or two, then water your box. The less sun your plants get, the less water they will need. When you do water, thoroughly drench the soil until water drips into your collection trays below.

Avoid temperatures below 40°F. Keep your box next to a sunny window during harsh winter months. A cold draft near a window is okay and often good for plants accustomed to cooler, but not freezing, temperatures.

Rotate your box to keep the succulents from leaning to one side.

plant with personality

- Thanks to the diversity of succulents, you can create a garden bursting with spreading, hanging greenery or keep it nice and tidy like a minimalist sculpture garden.

- To achieve pink tips, move your box outside in the summer months.

the
Ice Box

Even when the temperature drops, you can plant a box overflowing with greenery—plus some even juicier colors. The plants in this box are all freeze hardy (some can survive in temps as cold as −30°F) and include classics like a conifer and an ivy, and rising stars like ornamental kale. Plus there are some flashy surprises: pansies can remain in bloom through winter and into spring in cooler regions. In slushy cities like Washington, D.C., you might even see their striped faces mixed in with the snow.

LOCATION
Outdoors, hardy in USDA zones 2-11

LIGHT
High to medium

WINDOW
South-, east-, or west-facing

EASE
Intermediate

SOIL
Two parts potting soil, two parts pumice, one part compost

TOPPING
Cedar mulch

WATER
Once or twice per week, or whenever your pansies are slumping

FEED
16-16-16 fertilizer about once a month

A. *Chamaecyparis lawsoniana* 'Ellwoodii' (Lawson's cypress)

B. *Buxus sempervirens* (boxwood)

C. *Hedera helix* (English ivy)

D. *Viola* 'Mammoth Viva La Violet' (pansy)

E. *Viola* 'Matrix White' (pansy)

F. *Viola cornuta* 'Sorbet Citrus Mix' (viola)

G. *Ajuga reptans* 'Black Scallop' (common bugle)

H. *Brassica oleracea* var. *acephala* (ornamental kale)

1. Make sure your box has good drainage. If not, drill drain holes along the bottom of the box. Insert a screen cut to the size of the box's bottom to prevent soil from escaping or clogging the holes.

2. Mix the soil and add a healthy 3- to 4-inch layer to the bottom of the box.

3. Remove the plants from their containers and loosen the soil around the roots, breaking up any root-bound bundles. Arrange the plants on top of the soil 2–3 inches apart. Once the pansies are established, they'll start to spread!

4. Fill in the box with additional soil until the entire surface is level, and the bases of the plants are about 1 inch below the top of the planter. Feel free to gently adjust the plants until their bases line up across a smooth soil bed.

5. Top-dress the soil with cedar mulch.

Shower these cool-hearted beauties with kindness

Water when the first inch or so of soil is dry to the touch, roughly twice a week. Give your pansies a drink whenever they start to slump.

Expect your ivy and cypress to grow large, the former spreading horizontally and the latter gaining vertically. Gently uproot plants that have started to overtake the box; replant in the yard (if possible) or in their own larger container, or give them away to a friend.

During the summer, if the pansies and violas can no longer take the heat, bring in some annuals from the Edible Petals (page 96).

Make sure to give your plants a drink before any harsh freezes.

plant with personality

- For a classic look, hedge your grown-in boxwoods by cutting a straight line across the row at a full point near the top. You can also train your ivy to crawl up the facade of your building Spider Man—style to give your box a classic college-quad feeling.

- Add contrast to your box with complementary colors—in this case, purple and orange.

the
Detox Box

Thanks to their reputation for being rugged survivalists—able to stand tall in very low sunlight, even artificial lighting, and just about any kind of fast-draining soil—sansevieria (aka the snake plant or mother-in-law's tongue) has become a cliché plant in just about every office. But with its ubiquitous popularity, the true glamour of this trusty succulent has become lost. Across a range of cultures, the sansevieria has been associated with wealth, dragons, and protection from curses. On a more scientific note, snake plants were shown in a NASA Clean Air Study to remove benzene, formaldehyde, toluene, and other toxins from their surroundings. So plant this Detox Box and breathe easier!

* This box can also be grown outdoors. Avoid direct sunlight and make sure soil drains fully if it's watered by the rain. Plants are hardy outdoors in USDA zones 8b–11.

LOCATION
Indoors*

LIGHT
Low to medium (avoid direct sunlight)

WINDOW
North- or east-facing, or obstructed south- or west-facing

EASE
Very easy

SOIL
Two parts cactus mix, one part pumice

TOPPING
Jade pebbles

WATER
Low

FEED
Balanced liquid cactus fertilizer diluted to half strength two to three times a year

A. *Sansevieria suffruticosa*

B. *Sansevieria trifasciata* 'Golden Hahnii' (bird's-nest snake plant)

C. *Sansevieria masoniana* (Mason's Congo sansevieria)

D. *Sansevieria cylindrica* (African spear)

E. *Sansevieria trifasciata* 'Bantel's Sensation' (white-striped sansevieria)

F. *Sansevieria trifasciata* (snake plant)

TIP Strong pups (offsets) breaking through the soil is a sure sign your plants are happy.

1. Make sure your box has good drainage. If not, drill drain holes along the bottom of the box. Insert a screen cut to the size of the box's bottom to prevent soil from escaping or clogging the holes.

2. Mix the soil and add a healthy 3- to 4-inch layer to the bottom of the box.

3. Remove the plants from their containers and loosen the soil around the roots, breaking up any root-bound bundles. Arrange the plants on top of the soil. They have shallow root systems, so feel free to place your sansevierias within a few inches of each other.

4. Fill in the box with additional soil until the entire surface is level, and the bases of the plants are about 1 inch below the top of the planter.

5. Top-dress the soil with jade pebbles.

These stoic stunners have very few demands

When soil is dry to the touch, wait two weeks, then water. It's better to underwater than overwater; too many douses can reduce even the most resilient sansevieria to a yellow, mushy mess.

Do not pour water into the center of the rosette-shaped foliage. Water only the soil near the base of the plants, giving your box a healthy drench until the water flows out to the collection trays below.

Avoid temperatures below 50°F.

plant with personality

- In honor of the plants' sleek character, we painted our Detox Box glossy black.

- Surprisingly affordable jade "bean pebbles" and polished stones (about $9 per 3-pound bag) add an extra glow as top dressing.

- You can give the NASA Clean Air Study a nod by adding an astronaut figurine.

the Danglers

The leaves of the hoya are the main attraction of this box, with dramatically angled oval greenery, variegations like pink paint splatter, and, in the case of the Hindu rope, crumpled foliage that turns the plant into dangling strands of green scrunchies. (In our own garden, our variegated version has grown to 7 feet and counting.) Tired of plants outgrowing their containers? You'll love hoyas, which evolved to grow in crevices and other natural nooks; they actually bloom best when root-bound. Choose a shallow and narrow box to ensure the most blooms.

LOCATION
Indoors*

LIGHT
Medium to low

WINDOW
East- or north-facing, or shaded/obstructed south- or west-facing

EASE
Easy

SOIL
One part pumice, one part peat, one part bark

TOPPING
Clay pebbles

WATER
Medium

FEED
Balanced liquid fertilizer once a month in spring and summer

* You can also grow this box outside in USDA zones 10–12. Don't expose to direct sun or temps below 40°F.

A. *Hoya compacta* (Hindu rope)

B. *Hoya carnosa* 'Variegata' (variegated wax plant)

C. *Hoya obovata* (wax plant)

1. Make sure your box has good drainage. If not, drill drain holes along the bottom of the box. Insert a screen cut to the size of the box's bottom to prevent soil from escaping or clogging the holes.

2. If making a hanging box: Drill a ⅜-inch hole through the screen approximately 3 inches from each short edge. Secure two ¼ × 6-inch eyebolts with two sets of nuts and washers. Cut slits in the screen to accommodate the eyebolts. Install ceiling hooks to match the spacing of the planter eyebolts.

3. To plant the box: Mix the soil and add a healthy 3- to 4-inch layer to the bottom of the box.

4. Remove the plants from their containers and loosen the soil around the roots. Arrange the plants on top of the soil, spacing them evenly apart. Spread and untangle the vine stems; grow the vines on either side of the box or on both.

5. Fill in the box with additional soil until the entire surface is level, and the bases of the plants are about 1 inch below the top of the planter. Adjust the plants until their bases line up across a smooth soil bed. Top-dress the soil with clay pebbles.

6. Hang the planter box at the desired height with a decorative chain and S-hooks. Make sure your planter is easy to remove for watering.

Treat 'er right and a single hoya plant can thrive for decades

If your plant isn't blooming, it's probably not getting enough sunlight.

Be sure to keep the soil moist in spring and summer, while letting the soil go dry between waterings during winter.

Water the box in your sink or bathtub, giving it a good flush. Once most of the water is done dripping through the drain holes, move your box back to its hanging position or the sill.

Don't move the box while your plant is blooming, and do not remove the "spurs" that attach the blooms to the vine. Future rounds of blossoms use the same spurs! Let any faded flowers fall off on their own.

Rotate the box 180° or lower your hanging box if the vines aren't growing on both sides.

plant with personality

Best admired at eye level, these succulents love to
dangle. If hanging your garden from the ceiling isn't
an option, set your box on a high bookshelf, where the
vines can stylishly complement your favorite authors and
objects. Just be sure it's next to a bright window!

the Rain Forest

These luxuriously lush fronds scream "world traveler." After all, you'll find ferns under the waterfalls of Oregon and on the humid sidewalks of Singapore. They are forest lovers. They are tropical. They're in doctors' waiting rooms, and they even fed the stegosaurus. (First fossil records of ferns date back 360 million years ago, and estimates put today's existing number of species at about 13,000.) Ideal for indoors near a window exposed to indirect sun, the ferns of this box offer a chance to admire contrasting leaf shapes (and their coiled "fiddlehead" fronds-in-waiting) in all their glory.

---

* This box can also be grown outdoors. Avoid direct midday sun and opt for dappled light instead. Plants are hardy in USDA zone 9 and warmer.

LOCATION
Indoors*

LIGHT
Low to medium

WINDOW
East- or north-facing, or shaded south- or west-facing

EASE
Intermediate

SOIL
One part potting soil, two parts peat moss, one part orchid bark, one part pumice

TOPPING
Clay pebbles

WATER
High

FEED
A high-nitrogen fertilizer once a month from spring through early fall

A. *Pteris cretica* (ribbon fern)

B. *Nephrolepis exaltata* 'Fluffy Ruffles' (fluffy ruffle fern)

C. *Arachniodes simplicior* (East Indian holly fern)

D. *Nephrolepis obliterata* (sword fern)

E. *Asplenium nidus* (bird's-nest fern)

Platycerium bifurcatum (elkhorn fern; see page 94)

TIP Mist your ferns a couple times a week if your room is below 40 percent humidity.

1. Make sure your box has good drainage. If not, drill drain holes along the bottom of the box. Insert a screen cut to the size of the box's bottom to prevent soil from escaping or clogging the holes.

2. Mix the soil and add a healthy 3- to 4-inch layer to the bottom of the box.

3. Remove the plants from their containers and loosen the soil around the roots, breaking up any root-bound bundles. Arrange the plants on top of the soil.

4. Fill in the box with additional soil until the entire surface is level, and the bases of the plants are about 1 inch below the top of the planter. Feel free to gently adjust the plants until their bases line up across a smooth soil bed.

5. Top-dress the soil with clay pebbles.

Keep your ferns fluffy and green

Threatened by direct sun? Lower the blinds halfway to avoid frying your ferns.

Unlike the many drought-tolerant plants in this book, ferns do not want their soil to dry out between waterings. Make sure the soil stays evenly moist, but not waterlogged.

When a fern gets too big for the box, repot it in a larger container and replace it with a smaller fern. You can also divide a fern by taking a soil knife to the rhizomes or underground roots. (Research the technique before you slice!)

Snip off spent fronds for most ferns except elkhorn or staghorn ferns, whose long "fertile" fronds will fall off when they fade. But *do not* remove the dried shield-shaped fronds at the base—they protect the plant's roots, which support the plant.

plant with personality

- Embrace the '70s with a box that shows off its wood grain—like vintage basement paneling. We even added a couple coats of water-based spar urethane to enhance the grain.

- Elkhorn ferns and bird's-nest ferns prefer extra elbow room beyond what we could give them in a traditional long, cozy window box, so we made mini 10-inch-long boxes to accommodate their expansive lifestyle.

- Make your own plant stand by stacking painted concrete blocks. Add felt pads below the bottom block to prevent scratching hard floors.

the
Edible Petals

Ever see a flower that looked gorgeous enough to eat? While not all bodacious blooms are edible, the blossoms in this box are. From the peppery taste of nasturtium (excellent in fancy salads) to the honeyed bliss of alyssum on ice cream to the spectacle of dianthus frozen in your cocktail's ice cubes, edible flowers can add flavor, aroma, and color to your favorite dishes and drinks. This outdoor collection is a sun-loving one; a sunny, south-facing spot outdoors will encourage more petal production. This group of edible flowers prefers somewhat fertile soil with the exception of nasturtium, which blooms best in nutrient-deficient—yes, deficient—soil. Nasturtiums are also somewhat drought tolerant when established.

LOCATION
Outdoors; USDA zones 3–11

LIGHT
High to medium

WINDOW
South-, west-, or east-facing

EASE
Intermediate

SOIL
For the nasturtiums: two parts potting soil, one part coarse sand; for the rest: two parts potting soil, one part compost, one part pumice

TOPPING
Orchid bark or cedar mulch

WATER
See page 101

FEED
See page 101

A. *Tropaeolum majus* 'Wina' (Peach Melba nasturtium)

B. *Calendula officinalis*

C. *Pelargonium* 'Orange Fizz' (orange-scented geranium)

D. *Dianthus barbatus* (sweet william)

E. *Lobularia maritima* (alyssum)

F. *Lobularia maritima* 'Easter Bonnet Mix' (alyssum)

G. *Borago officinalis* (borage)

H. *Tagetes patula* 'Safari Bolero' (French dwarf marigold)

I. *Pelargonium* 'Attar of Roses' (rose-scented geranium)

J. *Tagetes erecta* (African marigold)

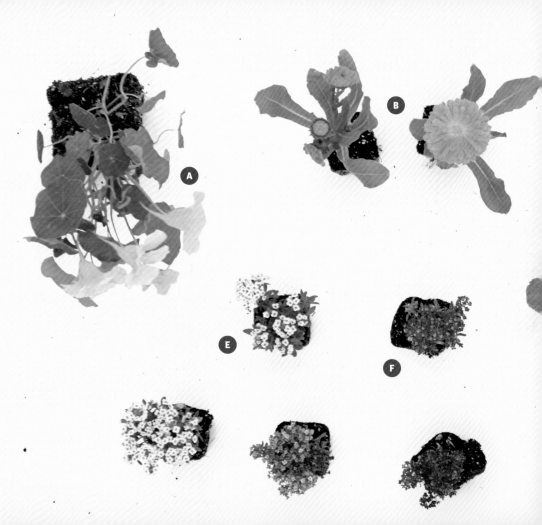

TIP To accommodate two different soil preferences, we added a wooden partition: Cut a piece of wood whose length is just shy of the depth of the box. Then just slide the piece into place. Make sure there is a drain hole below the new compartment.

1. Make sure your box has good drainage. If not, drill drain holes along the bottom of the box. Insert a screen cut to the size of the box's bottom to prevent soil from escaping or clogging the holes. Add a partition roughly 6 inches from the end of the box (see Tip).

2. Add the less-fertile soil/sand mix inside the smaller section of the box for the nasturtiums, and the soil/compost/pumice mix to the rest of the box. Pour in a 3- to 4-inch layer.

3. Remove the plants from their containers and loosen the soil around the roots, breaking up any root-bound bundles. Arrange the plants on top of the soil, spacing them closely, 1–2 inches apart.

4. Fill in the box with additional soil until the entire surface is level, and the bases of the plants are about 1 inch below the top of the planter. Top-dress the soil with orchid bark or cedar mulch.

KNOW BEFORE YOU NIBBLE An edible plant isn't necessarily safe to eat. This is especially true for flowers sold as ornamentals. Only use organic fertilizer and pesticides. Before you serve, rinse flowers thoroughly but gently. Snip off the anthers and stamens of your flower, to prevent allergic reactions. Also note that some edible flowers might have toxic foliage or are poisonous to pets (for example, dianthus).

Give your plants the (mari)gold standard of care

Expect your plants to die back when temperatures approach freezing.

Be diligent about snipping dead flowers and leaves, and trim back foliage that grows too shrubby for your taste. Shearing your alyssum after the first round of blooms will encourage a new round of vigorous flowering.

Marigolds are caterpillar targets, and calendula and dianthus are highly susceptible to powdery mildew. See page 27 for treatment options.

Use 10-10-10 fertilizer every few weeks in spring, summer, and fall for all plants but the nasturtiums. If the edges of your rose-scented geranium start to look burnt, reduce your fertilizer for this plant.

Water the nasturtiums once a week and the rest every few days.

plant with personality

- Pull out the paintbrush. An aubergine paint job (we used Behr's Vixen) will make your citrus-colored blossoms pop.

- Install a shelf to set a drink down while tending the garden or reading by your sill. Glue a grid of ⅝ × ⅝-inch dowels to rest across your window box.

the
Jungle Box

Want to hear one of the great ironies of the plant world? Tropical species that you associate with far-flung vacations can easily be enjoyed without leaving your house—even when you're snowed in! The pothos that drapes its gold-splashed vines below jungle canopies can shake up your bookshelf. The monstera, which has become fashionable for its holey, slashed leaves, adds an instant pattern to house facades and bright apartment windows alike. In this box, you can train your vines to climb a DIY grow pole and add tiki flair with a drop-down slatted shelf for your mister and tools. See page 110 for instructions.

---

* This box can also be grown outdoors. Avoid direct sunlight while seeking a spot that enjoys at least a few hours of bright (maybe dappled) light. These island beauties will likely survive winters only in USDA zone 10 and warmer.

LOCATION
Indoors*

LIGHT
Bright, indirect, filtered sunlight

WINDOW
East-facing or shaded/obstructed south- or west-facing

EASE
Difficult

SOIL
One part potting soil, one part pumice, one part peat moss

TOPPING
Lava rock

WATER
Moderate to high

FEED
A balanced fertilizer at half strength monthly from spring to fall

A. *Calathea lancifolia*
(rattlesnake plant)

B. *Alocasia amazonica* or *Alocasia*
'Polly' (elephant's ear)

C. *Epipremnum aureum* 'Golden
Pothos' (devil's ivy)

D. *Monstera deliciosa* (Swiss
cheese plant)

TIP We installed partitions to accommodate the different watering needs (see page 100 for instructions), but you could more easily exclude one or more plants to skip this step. We also kept the ivy in its pot to further protect its roots from overwatering.

1. Make sure your box has good drainage. If not, drill drain holes along the bottom of the box. Insert a screen cut to the size of the box's bottom to prevent soil from escaping or clogging the holes.

2. Add 2 soil partitions (see Tip) roughly 6–8 inches from the ends of the box.

3. Mix the soil and add a healthy 3- to 4-inch layer to the center section of the box.

4. Remove the elephant's ear and rattlesnake plant from their containers and loosen the soil around the roots, breaking up any root-bound bundles. Arrange them in the center section of the box, filling in the section with additional soil until the entire surface of the section is level.

5. Repeat steps 3 and 4 with the monstera in one end section of the box. Keeping the devil's ivy in its container, add it to the other end section, filling in the section with additional soil until the entire surface is level.

6. Top-dress the entire box with lava rock.

Ensure your garden is more than just a summer fling

These tropical beauties dig humidity, so in a dry climate, apply a fine mist a few times a week to the foliage. Even better, run a humidifier nearby.

Add some circulation—for example, from a fan or by opening the window—to make your plants even happier.

Repot if your plants get too big for their box.

Dust the leaves with a damp cloth so your leaves can bask in as much bright, filtered light as they can.

Some tropicals (the monstera and ivy) need to dry out between waterings while others (the elephant's ear and rattlesnake plant) like wet feet.

plant with personality

By gluing together a wood dowel grid (using the same technique as the DIY trellis on page 164) and connecting with hinges, mini eye hooks, and decorative chain, we customized our window box with a drop shelf. We then affixed a 1½ × 1½-inch square wood dowel to one end panel as a grow pole for the pothos.

the
Salad Bar

Join the "Grow Your Own" movement by cultivating kale, lettuce, and other leafy greens outside your windows. Your salads and sandwiches will be better than ever, thanks to your homegrown produce. These veggies are also packed with good-for-you nutrients, including vitamins K, A, and B_2, iron, zinc, dietary fiber, and calcium, and antioxidants like vitamin C. Hungry? Harvest the plants' outer leaves, clipping in the morning when crops are at their crispest and most hydrated.

LOCATION
Outdoors; USDA zones 2–11

LIGHT
High to medium

WINDOW
South-, west-, or east-facing

EASE
Intermediate

SOIL
Premixed soil dedicated to growing veggies

TOPPING
Compost, plus a top layer of orchid bark

WATER
High

FEED
Vegetable fertilizer every 10 to 14 days

A. *Lactuca sativa* 'Limestone Bibb' (Bibb lettuce)

B. *Lactuca sativa* 'Lollo Rossa Atsina' (curly red leaf lettuce)

C. *Beta vulgaris* subsp. *cicla* var. *flavescens* 'Bright Lights' (rainbow chard)

D. *Brassica oleracea* (Tuscan kale)

E. *Spinacia oleracea* (spinach)

TIP Because this box requires constant watering, we created our own irrigation system, but you can easily purchase self-watering window boxes online.

1. Make sure your box has good drainage. If not, drill drain holes along the bottom of the box. Insert a screen cut to the size of the box's bottom to prevent soil from escaping or clogging the holes.

2. Mix the soil and add it in an even layer until your box is halfway to two-thirds full. Remove the plants from their containers and loosen tightly wound roots (often the case for young leafy greens sold in six-packs) with your fingers. Plant the greens 2–4 inches apart, pressing each plant gently into the soil.

3. Fill in the box with additional soil until the entire surface is level, and the bases of the plants are about 1 inch below the top of the planter. Feel free to gently adjust the plants until their bases line up across a smooth soil bed.

4. Top-dress with a final layer of compost and orchid bark.

Greens are good for you, so return the favor

Place the window box on a sunny south- or west-facing side of your home. These plants love the cooler weather of spring and fall. In milder climates, your greens can also be a delicious winter crop; the same goes for colder climates if a protective covering is used.

When the weather heats up, the plants will "bolt," sending out flower stalks so the plant can go to seed. (You could try to delay this stage by providing your box with some shade from the summer sun.) Bolting leads to bitter leaves, so harvest your greens ASAP.

Don't let your garden dry out! Maintain moist—but not waterlogged—soil.

plant with personality

- Paint your box a clay color to mimic earthy terra-cotta.
- Apply a layer of orchid bark for a clean look and to retain soil moisture.

the Flower Stand

Celebrate the arrival of warm breezes and longer days with a box full of your favorite blooms. This box brings together some of the classic first flowers to appear in late winter through spring, including daffodils, tulips, and ranunculuses. These blossoms can be short-lived, so we planted an iris for late-season flash, plus a second round of asters, foxgloves, and delphiniums. Embedded vase holders for cut flowers—including fluffy favorites like peonies—are an unexpected way to keep the fair-weather vibes flowing.

LOCATION
Outdoors; USDA zones 4–10

LIGHT
High to medium

WINDOW
South-, west-, or east-facing

EASE
Intermediate

SOIL
Two parts potting soil, one part pumice, one part compost

TOPPING
Cedar mulch

WATER
Moderate to high

FEED
Low-nitrogen food—e.g., 5-10-10 or 3-5-3—every 2 to 3 weeks while flowering

EARLY-SPRING BLOOMERS

A. *Narcissus* 'Mount Hood' (trumpet daffodil)

B. *Tulipa gesneriana* (garden tulip)

C. *Ranunculus asiaticus*

D. *Iris germanica* 'Autumn Encore' (bearded iris)

LATE-SPRING BLOOMERS

E. *Thymophylla tenuiloba* (Dahlberg daisy)

F. *Chrysanthemum leucanthemum* (oxeye daisy)

not shown:

G. *Digitalis purpurea* (foxglove)

H. *Delphinium elatum* 'Pacific Giant Galahad' (alpine delphinium or candle larkspur)

1. If adding vase holders, see page 126 before proceeding. Make sure your box has good drainage. If not, drill drain holes along the bottom of the box. Insert a screen cut to the size of the box's bottom to prevent soil from escaping or clogging the holes.

2. Mix the soil and add a healthy 3- to 4-inch layer to the bottom of the box.

3. Remove the plants from their containers and loosen the soil around the roots, breaking up any root-bound bundles. Arrange the plants on top of the soil, spacing them closely, 1–2 inches apart.

4. Fill in the box with additional soil until the entire surface is level, and the bases of the plants are about 1 inch below the top of the planter. Feel free to gently adjust the plants until their bases line up across a smooth soil bed. Top-dress the soil with cedar mulch.

5. When the flowers fade, pull up the plants and dig up the bulbs. Discard or add to a compost pile, if you have one. Repeat steps 3 and 4 with the late-spring-blooming plants.

THE BRIGHTEST BULBS Missed the bulb-planting bus in the fall? Don't worry—this box uses budding and flowering plants found in nurseries in late winter and early spring.

Get your blooms to petal harder, faster, stronger

Water after first planting; this goes for bulbs and grown plants alike. Then water whenever the first inch of soil feels dry, about once every two or three days.

Most of the flowers in this box can be perennial in select climates; see page 21. Daffodils, in particular, are reliable rebloomers if you let the foliage die back on its own and leave the bulb in the ground, even when it's supposed to snow.

Keep the box tidy and blooming by snipping off spent flowers and faded leaves.

plant with personality

We made vase holders to display cut spring flowers once they're no longer available as potted plants. It's also a smart way to add color to your box while you are waiting for your plants to bloom. Here's an easy two-step process:

1. Cut 2-inch PVC piping with a handsaw to the height of your box. Add a PVC pipe cap to the bottom and place the vase holder(s) in the box before adding soil.

2. Arrange cut flowers in a 1³/₄-inch diameter glass vase, add water, and insert the glass vase into the PVC holder. When not in use, cover the top end of the vase holder with another pipe cap to prevent it from filling up with standing water.

the
Woodlands

Take an enchanted walk through the forest with a collection of plants that thrive in a cool, partially shaded area of your home's exterior. In this mini garden, leaves with interesting textures mingle with foliage in unexpected colors, bringing sizzle to low-light settings. Quirky but exuberant flowers add star power.

Hostas (also known as plantain lilies) might seem unassuming at first, but this shade-loving genus enjoys an immense global fan club—particularly in Britain. Devotees are drawn to the plants' grooved, fantastically variegated leaves, abundance of sizes, and stalks of elegant and sometimes fragrant flowers. There are hosta hybrids named for famous people, everyone from Marilyn Monroe and tennis player Andy Murray to King Tut and Prince Charles, who grows them in his Highgrove House garden; the 'Prince of Wales' hosta can reach upward of 4 feet wide!

LOCATION
Outdoors, USDA zones 2–9

LIGHT
Medium (indirect dappled sunlight)

WINDOW
East- or north-facing, obstructed south- or west-facing

EASE
Intermediate

SOIL
Two parts peat moss, two parts medium orchid bark, one part pumice

TOPPING
Cedar mulch

WATER
Moderate to high

FEED
10-10-10 fertilizer once in spring

A. *Saxifraga fortunei* 'Pink Elf' (saxifrage)

B. *Aquilegia × hybrida* 'Origami Yellow' (columbine)

C. *Hosta* 'Abiqua Drinking Gourd'

D. *Dicentra* 'Luxuriant' (fringed bleeding heart)

E. *Heuchera* 'Frosted Violet' (coral bells)

F. *Heuchera* 'Dolce Creme Brulee' (coral bells)

G. *Hosta* 'Minuteman'

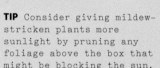

1. Make sure your box has good drainage. If not, drill drain holes along the bottom of the box. Insert a screen cut to the size of the box's bottom to prevent soil from escaping or clogging the holes.

2. Mix the soil and add a healthy 3- to 4-inch layer to the bottom of the box.

3. Remove the plants from their containers and loosen the soil around the roots, breaking up any root-bound bundles. Arrange the plants on top of the soil, spacing them about 3 inches apart.

4. Fill in the box with additional soil until the entire surface is level, and the bases of the plants are about 1 inch below the top of the planter. Feel free to gently adjust the plants until their bases line up across a smooth soil bed.

5. Top-dress the soil with cedar mulch.

"Wood" you please

Prune spent leaves. Deadhead any flowers before they develop seedpods; this will redirect the plants' energy to its leaves.

Feel free to gently uproot volunteers (unplanned seedlings from parent plants) and transfer them to another container.

If slugs are a threat, add a strip or two of copper tape around the outside of your box to deter them; or sprinkle some diatomaceous earth around your hostas. Slugs will go out of their way to avoid its scratchy texture.

Maintain evenly moist soil.

plant with personality

- Add even more magic to your Woodlands box by turning it into a "stumpery," a garden style centered around bringing life to dead tree parts. Place small stumps, logs, and driftwood in artful arrangements among your plants.

- Allow some room for these plants to grow; we mixed together tall and short specimens so that we could squeeze in a whopping seven plants in this box. We also liked playing with the diversity of leaf textures and colors.

the Beach Dune

In landscaping, just a few tufts of decorative grass—separated by stones, concrete pavers, or bark mulch—can go a long way in creating a statement. Inspired by the urban-meadow High Line in New York and other modern grasslands of garden designer Piet Oudolf, this window box tickles the senses with just a handful of noninvasive pom-poms in dramatic colors and irresistible textures.

Make sure the grass you choose isn't invasive, especially if you're thinking of planting outside the box. Creepy culprits—like pampas, lilyturf, and maidenhair grass—and certain species of fountain grass can push out native plants. Even from inside a window box, seeds from weedy greenery can travel in the wind and wreak havoc on your local ecosystem.

LOCATION
Outdoors; USDA zones 6–11

LIGHT
High

WINDOW
South-, east-, or west-facing

EASE
Intermediate

SOIL
Cactus/succulent mix

TOPPING
Salt-free horticultural sand or a coarse washed silica sand

WATER
Moderate

FEED
10-10-10 fertilizer only once in spring (if at all)

A. *Juncus effusus* 'Quartz Creek'
(soft rush)

B. *Pennisetum* 'Fireworks' (purple
fountain grass)

C. *Carex testacea* 'Prairie Fire'
(New Zealand hair sedge)

D. *Zephyranthes candida* (fairy lily)

E. *Festuca glauca* (blue fescue)

TIP Keep plants watered and fed appropriately as a natural defense against opportunistic bugs like aphids and mites.

1. Make sure your box has good drainage. If not, drill drain holes along the bottom of the box. Insert a screen cut to the size of the box's bottom to prevent soil from escaping or clogging the holes.

2. Mix the soil and add a healthy 3- to 4-inch layer to the bottom of the box.

3. Remove the plants from their containers and loosen the soil around the roots, breaking up any root-bound bundles. Arrange the plants on top of the soil, leaving a couple inches of space between plants.

4. Fill in the box with additional soil until the entire surface is level, and the bases of the plants are about 1 inch below the top of the planter.

5. Top-dress the soil with salt-free horticultural sand or a coarse washed silica sand.

Protect your turf

Feel free to prune flowers from fescue to maintain neat, energetic grass clumps.

Divide plants that get too big for your box. Many videos online can show you the best technique.

These plants aren't heavy feeders. If you really want, apply controlled-release granules to the top few inches of soil in the spring.

Cut back dried blades in very late winter or early spring in plants that went dormant (this could mean a drastic haircut!); in the case of small evergreen grasses like sedge, gently comb through the plant to remove spent foliage. Do this using your hands while wearing sturdy gloves, which will protect you from getting cut by the plant's sharp blades.

plant with personality

- For a modern take on the classic American lawn, add mini pink flamingos to your box. We easily found a pair at our local nursery!

- Put the two tallest plants on the ends, then alternate tall and short plants in the middle. Or create a color gradient. As plants get established, expect them to grow closer together to create an East Coast beach vibe.

the
Southern Belle

Some of the most iconic window boxes in the United States can be found in New Orleans and Charleston, where containers overflow with cascades of vines (like sweet potato or ivy) flanked by plants that fill their spaces with psychedelic leaves and cheeky flowers. Height is another key to the formula: In New Orleans, huge orbs of ferns dangle in midair above over-the-top railing gardens. In Charleston, boxes are crowned by eye-catchers like cordyline, foxglove, snapdragon, and caladium. This arrangement follows the tried-and-true thriller/spiller/filler formula: thrillers are your tall centerpiece plants, spillers cascade over the side, and fillers are mounding plants that give your box a look of volume and fullness.

LOCATION
Outdoors; USDA zones 7–12

LIGHT
High

WINDOW
South-, west-, or east-facing

EASE
Intermediate

SOIL
One part potting soil, one part pumice, one part compost

TOPPING
None

WATER
High

FEED
A balanced, controlled-release granular fertilizer as directed in spring

A. *Pentas lanceolata* 'Graffiti Lavender'

B. *Ipomoea* 'SolarPower Black' (sweet potato vine)

C. *Calibrachoa Calitastic* 'Pumpkin Spice'

D. *Plectranthus coleoides* 'Variegata' (variegated Swedish ivy)

E. *Senecio cineraria* (dusty miller)

F. *Lysimachia nummularia* (creeping jenny)

TIP In colder climates, save your sweet potato vine at the end of the season. Cut 12- to 18-inch strands, rinse off excess soil, remove the lower leaves, and place the stems in a glass jar with water near a bright window. Plant the rooted cuttings outside in the spring.

1. This box needs a lot of water. If your box is wood, we recommend installing a plastic liner to preserve its life (see page 162). Drill holes every 6 inches to ensure the box has excellent drainage.

2. Mix the soil and add a healthy 3- to 4-inch layer to the bottom of the box.

3. Remove the plants from their containers and loosen the soil around the roots, breaking up any root-bound bundles. Arrange the plants on top of the soil, symmetrically, spacing 2–3 inches apart. Feel free to pack in the plants to create a full box. Line the front of the box with spillers, placing fillers behind them, and thrillers in the back.

4. Plant in this order: spillers, fillers, and thrillers. Fill in the box with additional soil until the entire surface is level, and the bases of the plants are about 1 inch below the top of the planter.

Keep these steel magnolias from wilting

Assemble plants that work best in your environment, have similar needs, and, of course, strike your fancy.

Keep the soil moist by watering every other day. As this box is packed full of plants, make sure to water across the entire surface, and don't let the soil dry out and harden between waterings. The best method is to water from outside with a hose, or better yet, use a timed irrigation system or self-watering box.

Deadhead spent flowers and leaves.

plant with personality

For our Southern Belle flora, we broke from our modernist style and added classic trim to the container. Here's how:

1. Cut 2-inch trim board with a handsaw into 12 pieces: 4 pieces that run the length of the box, 4 pieces that run the inside width of the box, and 4 pieces that run the height of the box.

2. Using wood glue and 1¼-inch finishing nails, glue and nail the pieces to the outside of the box.

3. Sand and paint the box as desired.

the
Window Bog

This box is a challenge. But success comes down to four key factors: proper soil (potting soil is fatal to carnivorous plants), the right kind (and amount) of water, lots of sunlight, and dormancy, which we'll explain in a minute. The fact is, you can't beat the thrill of watching a Venus flytrap closing in on its prey. Find high-quality carnivorous plants at specialized nurseries, carnivorous plant shows, and reputable online sources like CaliforniaCarnivores.com. The most iconic carnivorous plant might be the toothy green spell caster that is the Venus flytrap (thanks, *Little Shop of Horrors*), but there's a whole bloodthirsty world of bug-eating plants out there. The carnivores we're planting hunt best in the bright, damp, humid conditions found in their native bogs.

LOCATION
Outdoors; USDA zones 8-10

LIGHT
High

WINDOW
South- or west-facing

EASE
Difficult

SOIL
For the sundew section: two parts sphagnum peat moss, one part coarse silica sand, one part rinsed perlite; for the flytrap and sarracenia section: all long-fiber sphagnum moss

TOPPING
None

WATER
Very high (see page 157)

FEED
Live insects, once or twice a week at most

A. *Drosera filiformis* var. *filiformis* 'Florida Giant' (sundew)

B. *Sarracenia* × 'Abandoned Hope' (pitcher plant)

C. *Sarracenia* 'Scarlet Belle' (pitcher plant)

D. *Sarracenia leucophylla* 'Tarnok' (pitcher plant)

E. *Dionaea muscipula* 'Red Dragon' (Venus flytrap)

F. *Dionaea muscipula* (Venus flytrap)

G. *Drosera filiformis* var. 'Tall Paul' (sundew)

H. *Drosera binata* (forked-leaf sundew)

I. *Drosera capensis* (Cape sundew)

1. Create a bog environment in your box (see page 170) with a constant water level of 1–2 inches in the bottom of the box.

2. Mix and moisten soil ingredients with distilled water. Use gloves when mixing the long-fiber sphagnum moss.

3. Install one partition in the middle of the box (see page 100). Fill the sundew side with peat-sand-perlite mix, and the pitcher plant and flytrap side with long-fiber sphagnum moss.

4. Form narrow holes in the soil with your fingers and insert the plants. Fill in with soil. Water immediately until you see water draining from the raised drainage tubes.

LET'S FLY AWAY To catch a live fly, stun it first lightly with a swatter. Place the wiggling insect inside your flytrap. Feeding a flytrap more than twice a week will not lead to bigger traps, so don't overfeed it.

There's a reason why Audrey II is so demanding

Avoid watering with tap or bottled water, which are full of dissolved mineral salts that will kill these plants. Use collected rainwater, reverse osmosis (the kind found at fill stations outside of supermarkets), or distilled water.

Maintain moist, well-draining soil by watering once or twice a week until water flows out of the drains. Never let the top level of soil dry out completely. If a fungal breakout happens (dark spores on foliage, collapsing greenery), improve circulation and light exposure and replace your soil.

Fertilizing is not recommended. If you feel like plant growth is flagging, try lightly dampening the foliage with an orchid/epiphyte foliar spray diluted to one-fourth strength.

Most of your plants will go dormant in the winter. Keep them cooler—between 40°F and 55°F at night—and exposed to a shorter photoperiod. In freezing winter temps, stash the box in the coolest unheated area of the house with some natural light (like the garage near a window). Don't worry about feeding.

plant with personality

The reddish stain we used on this box adds drama to
this garden, while the grain plays off of the veiny
variegations of the pitcher plants.

Customize Your Box

Lining Your Box

1. Measure the complete inside length and width of your box (A).

2. Mark this measurement on the plastic sheeting and cut out the liner (B).

3. Insert the liner into the box (C), folding the plastic at the ends as necessary to fit the liner and cover all sides of the box's interior (D).

4. Staple the liner around the top edge of the box (E).

5. If your box has no drainage holes, drill up to three large drain holes in the bottom of the box, keeping in mind where you want to position the water collection trays (F). If your box has holes, simply cut away the plastic at the holes.

6. For best results, glue the two wood strips to the outside bottom of the box and insert water collection trays beneath the box to collect water that drains.

YOU WILL NEED

Tape measure

Framing square (optional)

Plastic sheeting (small drop sheet or a large thick garbage bag)

Scissors

Staple gun

Drill with ⅜-inch drill bit

Wood glue (optional)

Two 1-inch wood strips cut to the width of your box (optional)

TIP Installing a soft liner is a great way to make any wood box suitable for indoor use or for preserving the life of an outdoor box. If you're confident that the box is already leakproof and can withstand moist soil, then simply caulking the interior joints and seams of the box with a marine waterproof sealant (we love Loctite) will make it water resistant. Make sure the box has adequate holes at the bottom for drainage. You may need to drill them yourself.

Add a Trellis
the tiny island box (page 48)

1. Using a transparent ruler, mark slat guidelines on the upright posts: there should be 1 inch of space between the slats (A).

2. On a flat surface (add paper for protection from the glue) loosely arrange the trellis. Using a tape measure or a framing square, space the upright posts parallel to each other so that the inner edge distance is equal to the outer edges of the window box end panels. Place the support strips at about 8 inches inside of the upright posts.

3. Apply beads of glue at the markings on the upright posts (B). Place the horizontal slats across the upright posts on the glue and across the support strips. Ensure the slats are perpendicular to the posts while the glue is still wet; for best results, use a framing square and a wood strip as a spacer (C).

4. Carefully place the concrete blocks over the slats to add pressure while the glue dries for at least 24 hours (D). Once the glue has dried, sand and apply paint, oil, or beeswax to preserve the wood.

5. Attach the trellis to the back edge of the end panels, 2 inches from the top of the window box, with the screws; predrill the posts with the ⅛-inch diameter drill bit so that the wood does not split when fastening the screws (E).

YOU WILL NEED

Transparent ruler

Two ⅝ × ⅝-inch square wood dowels for posts cut to 20 inches (or desired height)

Five ¾ × ¼-inch horizontal trellis slats cut to the outside width of the window box (see Tip)

Tape measure

Framing square (optional)

Two ⅝ × ⅝-inch square wood dowels for support strips cut to about 10 inches

Wood glue

Two concrete blocks or other flat heavy objects

120-grit sandpaper and paint, oil, or beeswax, as desired

Drill with ⅛-inch drill bit

Two #6 × 1¼-inch screws

Screwdriver

One wood strip cut to the distance between posts for a spacer (optional)

TIP Look for screen molding at your local hardware store, and feel free to change up the dimensions of the slats depending on material availability and your aesthetic.

Add Grow Lights
the herb garden box (page 40)

1. **Make the arbor:** Glue four long wood slats spaced ⅝ inch apart to the two straps to create a grid. Space the straps to match the width of the box.

2. **Make the adjustable uprights:** Starting ¾ inch from the top, drill eight ¼-inch holes through the uprights every 1½ inches. Predrill two 1/16-inch holes 1 inch and 4 inches from the bottom (A).

3. Sand and apply paint, stain, or oil to the trellis and uprights as desired. Attach the uprights to the side of the box with two screws per side where you predrilled the two holes.

4. **Attach the grow lights:** Remove the tape that comes attached to the strips. For extra hold, apply rubber cement to attach the strips to the underside of the trellis (B).

5. **Mount the arbor:** Slide the arbor between the upright posts and drill ¼-inch holes through the post hole and straps at each end. Slip in the eyebolts at a height just above the tallest leaves of the plants (C).

6. Connect the lights following the manufacturer's instructions. If desired, plug the outlet timer into a wall outlet, then plug the LED adapter into the outlet timer (D). Program the outlet to turn on for 12 to 14 hours per day.

YOU WILL NEED

Wood glue and rubber cement

Four ¼ × ⅝-inch wood slats cut to the length of the box

Two ⅝ × ⅝-inch square wood dowels cut to the width of the box straps

Drill with 1/16-inch and ¼-inch drill bits

Two ⅝ × ⅝ × 18½-inch square wood dowels

Paint, stain, or oil (optional)

Four #6 × 1¼-inch wood screws

Screwdriver

12V Flexible LED grow light strip kit with power adapter (see Tip)

Two 3/16 × 2-inch steel eyebolts

24-hour mechanical outlet timer

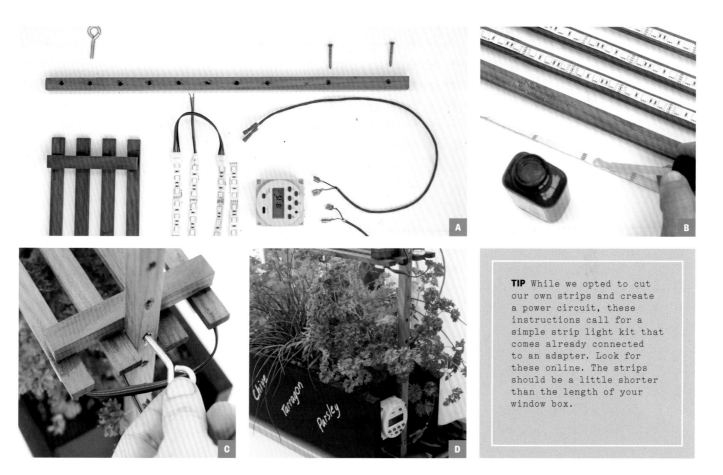

TIP While we opted to cut our own strips and create a power circuit, these instructions call for a simple strip light kit that comes already connected to an adapter. Look for these online. The strips should be a little shorter than the length of your window box.

Create a Bog
the window bog (page 152)

1. Using clippers, cut the tubing in half so that you have two 3-inch lengths.

2. Place the liner in the window box and measure 2 inches from each end, marking these places with masking tape. Drill two ⅜-inch holes through the bottom of the liner and the wood at the 2-inch marks (A). Remove the tape and rough up the holes in the plastic liner with sandpaper (B).

3. Insert the plastic drainage tubes through each hole so that 1½–2 inches of the tubing pokes through the liner (C). There should be just under ½ inch of tube sticking out below the bottom panel. If needed, remove and trim the tubes with the clippers as required to achieve these heights.

4. Sand the outside of each tube and fit it back in the box at the final height, making sure both tubes are even to each other. Wipe surfaces with a damp cloth and apply sealant around the tube penetration. Wearing a latex glove, smooth the bead of sealant with your finger (D). Allow 24 hours to dry.

5. Fill the box with 1 inch of water to test for leakage before adding soil and plants (E).

YOU WILL NEED

Gardening clippers or sharp scissors

¼-inch (⅜-inch outer diameter) × 6 inches polyethylene tubing

Plastic liner to fit the inside of your box (see Tip)

Tape measure

Masking tape

Drill with ⅜-inch drill bit

80-grit sandpaper

Small tube silicone sealant

Latex glove

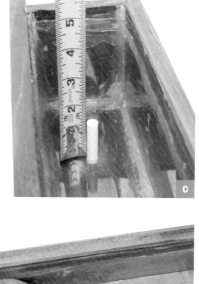

TIP For a cleaner look, we opted to create our own liner by cutting acrylic sheeting to fit the inside dimensions of our box and sealing the pieces together with silicone sealant.

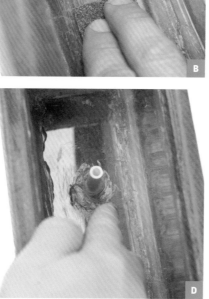

Resources

WHERE TO BUY PLANTS

Air Plant Shop,
airplantshop.com

Altman Plants,
altmanplants.com/plant-shop

American Meadows,
americanmeadows.com

Annie's Annuals,
anniesannuals.com

Armstrong Garden Centers,
armstronggarden.com

Brent and Becky's,
brentandbeckysbulbs.com

California Carnivores,
californiacarnivores.com

Ebay,
ebay.com

Etsy,
etsy.com

Georgia Vines,
georgiavines.com

Home Depot,
homedepot.com

Logee's,
logees.com

Lowes,
lowes.com

Monrovia,
monrovia.com

Old House Gardens Heirloom Bulbs,
oldhousegardens.com

Pigment,
shoppigment.com

Plant Oddities,
plantoddities.com

The Sill,
thesill.com

Theodore Payne Foundation,
theodorepayne.org

Tropiflora,
tropiflora.com

Plus: Plant shows, plant clubs (like The Cactus and Succulent Society of America, CSSA), and your local independent nurseries and garden centers, of course!

WHERE TO LEARN MORE ABOUT PLANTS (INCLUDING CARE ESSENTIALS!)

Books & Magazines

Air Plants: The Curious World of Tillandsias by Zenaida Sengo

Better Homes & Gardens magazine

The Complete Houseplant Survival Manual: Essential Know-How for Keeping (Not Killing) More Than 160 Indoor Plants by Barbara Pleasant

Country Gardens magazine

The Encyclopedia of Herbs: A Comprehensive Reference to Herbs of Flavor and Fragrance by Arthur O. Tucker and Thomas DeBaggio

Garden Design magazine

Gardening for Geeks by Christy Wilhelmi

Good Bug Bad Bug: Who's Who, What They Do, and How to Manage Them Organically by Jessica Walliser

Grow Great Grub: Organic Food from Small Spaces by Gayla Trail

Indoor Edible Garden by Zia Allaway

Kiss My Aster: A Graphic Guide to Creating a Fantastic Yard Totally Tailored to You by Amanda Thomsen

The New Western Garden Book: The Ultimate Gardening Guide by Editors of *Sunset* magazine

The Savage Garden, Revised: Cultivating Carnivorous Plants by Peter D'Amato

Slow Flowers: Four Seasons of Locally Grown Bouquets from the Garden, Meadow and Farm by Debra Prinzing

Succulents Simplified: Growing, Designing, and Crafting with 100 Easy-Care Varieties by Debra Lee Baldwin

Sunset magazine

The Timber Press Guide to Succulent Plants of the World: A Comprehensive Reference to More Than 2000 Species by Fred Dortort

Urban Jungle: Living and Styling with Plants by Igor Josifovic and Judith de Graaff

A Way to Garden: A Hands-On Primer for Every Season by Margaret Roach

Online

Almanac.com/gardening

AWaytoGarden.com

BHG.com/gardening

Bromeliads.info

Davesgarden.com

DebraLeeBaldwin.com/succulent-blog

Extension.missouri.edu

FlyTrapCare.com

GardenBetty.com

Gardenerd.com

GardeningKnowHow.com

HGTV.com

HomeGuides.SFGate.com/gardening

Houseplant411.com

HouseplantJournal.com

JoyUsGarden.com

Penick.net/digging

TheHorticult.com (Check out our other DIY projects, including how to build your own box.)

Acknowledgments

This book couldn't have bloomed without the care of wonderful people. Thank you to our extraordinary agent, Meredith Kaffel Simonoff, for her sage and powerhouse guidance; to our ingenious editor, Angelin Borsics, for her irresistible vision for gardening anywhere; and to Ian Dingman for giving our book a look and feel beyond our wildest dreams. To Kathy Brock for her spectacular attention to detail, and to Nicole Ramirez, Kim Tyner, Carolyn Gill, and Erin Voigt at Potter. To Tim King for his photographic savvy and assistance. We're also grateful to Pigment boutique, Carol Domanick, David Deitch, Debra Prinzing, Warren Keller, Jill Blumenthal, Michael Tortorello, Laura Joliet, Jacqueline Bonelli Smith, Tina and Craig Stern, Stephen Orr, James A. Baggett, and the brilliant *BHG* team, Jim Peterson and the stars onboard *Garden Design*, Green Gardens Nursery, Tiffany J. Davis, Jennifer Gilbert Asher, Julian Mackler, Anthony Rossi, Clity Gordon, Godfrey Gordon, Denise and Robert Benoit, Warren Wilson's MFA Program for Writers, and to the readers of *The Horticult*, for their gardening wisdom, enthusiasm, and evergreen curiosity.

Index

A

African marigold, 98
African spear, 74
Air plants, 48–55
Alpine delphinium, 122
Alyssum, 98, 101
Aphids, 140
Asters, 121

B

Baby necklace, 58
The Beach Dune, 136–43
Bearded iris, 122
Bibb lettuce, 114
Bird's-nest fern, 90, 94
Bird's-nest snake plant, 74
Blue fescue, 138
Blushing bromeliad, 50
Bog, creating a, 170–71
Borage, 98
Boxes
    adding brackets to, 162–63
    adding grow lights to, 168–69
    adding trellis to, 166–67
    buying plants for, 20–21
    considerations for, 14–15
    creating bog in, 170–71
    hardiness zones, 18–19
    indoor, adding liner to, 164–65
    soil mediums for, 22
    sunlight for, 17–18
    surface styles for, 23
    tools for, 20
Boxwood, 66, 70

Brackets, for boxes, 162–63
Bromeliads, 48–55
Burro's tail, 58

C

Cache potting, 28
Cactaceae family, 33
Cacti, 32–39
Cactus/succulent soil mix, 22
Calendula, 101
Candle larkspur, 122
Cape sundew, 155
Carnivorous plants, 152–59
Caterpillars, 101
Cedar mulch, 23
Chard, 114
Chives, 42
Cilantro, 42, 45
Clay pebbles, 23
Coarse sand, 23
Columbine, 130
Common bugle, 66
Compost, 22
Cone-headed guzmania, 50
Coppertone stonecrop, 58
Coral bells, 130
Creeping jenny, 146
Crested bird's-nest fern, 90
Curly red leaf lettuce, 114
Cypress, 66, 69

D

Daffodils, 122, 125
Dahlberg daisy, 122
Daisies, 122
The Danglers, 80–87
Delphiniums, 122
The Detox Box, 72–79
Devil's ivy, 106
Dianthus, 101
Diatomaceous earth (D.E.), 28
Dusty miller, 146

E

East Indian holly fern, 90
The Edible Petals, 96–103
Elephant food, 58
Elephant's ear, 106
Elkhorn fern, 90, 93, 94
English ivy, 28, 66
Euphorbias, 32–39

F

Fairy lily, 138
Ferns, 88–95
Fertilizers, 26–27, 28, 101
Flamingos, pink, 142
Flaming sword, 50
Flowers
    edible, 96–103
    faded, pinching off, 68
    making vase holders for, 126
The Flower Stand, 120–27
Fluffy ruffle fern, 90
Forked leaf sundew, 155

Foxglove, 122
French dwarf marigold, 98
Fringed bleeding heart, 130
Fungal infections, 27

G

Garden tulip, 122
Geraniums, 98
Golden barrel cactus, 34
Grasses, decorative, 136–43
Greens leafy, 112–19
Grow lights, creating, 168–69

H

Hardiness zones, 19
The Herb Garden, 40–47
Hindu rope, 82
Horticultural sand, 22
Hostas, 130
Hoyas, 80–87

I

The Ice Box, 64–71
Irises, 28, 122
Ivies, 28, 66, 69, 70, 109

J

Jade bean pebbles, 23
Jelly bean plant, 58
The Jungle Box, 104–11

K

Kale, 114

L
Lava rock, 23
Lawson's cypress, 66
Lettuce, 114
Long-fiber sphagnum moss, 22

M
Marigolds, 98, 101
Mason's Congo sansevieria, 74
Mites, 140
Monstera, 103, 106, 109

N
NASA Clean Air Study, 73
Nasturtiums, 98
Neem oil, 27
New Zealand hair sedge, 138
Nitrogen, 26
NPK, 26

O
Orange-scented geranium, 98
Orchid bark, 22, 23
Oregano, 42
Ornamental kale, 66
Oxeye daisy, 122

P
Paddle plant, 58
Panda plant, 58
Pansies, 66, 69
Parsley, 42, 45
Peach melba nasturtium, 98
Perlite, 22

Pest control, 27
Pesticides, 101
Phosphorus, 26
Pink flamingos, 142
Pitcher plants, 155
Plants
  annuals, 21
  biennials, 21
  buying, 20–21
  cache potting, 28
  fertilizing, 26–27
  Latin and common names, 21
  perennials, 21
  pest control, 27
  pruning, 27
  replacing, 27
  root systems, 24
  soil mediums for, 22
  soil mixes for, 24
  watering, 25, 28
Poisonous plants, 28
Polished pebbles, 23
Potassium, 26
Pothos, 103
Potting soil, 22
Powdery mildew, 27, 101
Pumice, 22
Purple fountain grass, 138

R
Rainbow chard, 114
The Rainforest, 88–95
Ranunculus, 121, 122
Rattlesnake plant, 106

Ribbon fern, 90
Rose-scented geranium, 98, 101

S
Sage, 42, 45
The Salad Bar, 112–19
The Sand Box, 32–39
Sansevieria, 72–79
Saxifrage, 130
Scarlet star, 50
Slugs, 133
Snake plant, 74
Soft rush, 138
Soils and soil mixes, 22, 24
The Southern Belle, 144–51
Sphagnum peat moss, 22
Spinach, 114
Staghorn ferns, 93
Stonecrop, 58
Stumps, 134
Succulents
  for The Detox Box, 72–79
  propagating, 61
  for The Sand Box, 32–39
  for The Sunny Succulents, 56–63
Succulent soil mix, 22
Sundews, 155
Sunlight, 17–18, 19
The Sunny Succulents, 56–63
Sweet potato vine, 146, 148
Sweet william, 98
Swiss cheese plant, 106
Sword fern, 90

T
Tarragon, 28, 42
Thyme, 42, 45
The Tiny Island, 48–55
Tools, 20
Toxic plants, 28
Tree stumps, 134
Trellis, adding to box, 166–67
Trumpet daffodil, 122
Tulips, 122
Tuscan kale, 114

U
USDA zones, 19

V
Variegated Swedish ivy, 146
Variegated wax plant, 82
Venus flytrap, 155, 157
Vines, 144–51
Violas, 66, 69

W
Wax plant, 82
Weather conditions, 18–19
White-striped sansevieria, 74
The Window Bog, 152–59
The Woodlands, 128–36

Library of Congress
LC record is available at
https://lccn.loc.gov/2017044896.

ISBN 978-1-5247-6024-3
Ebook ISBN 978-1-5247-6025-0

Book and cover design by
Ian Dingman
Interior and cover photographs by
Ryan Benoit
Endpaper illustration by
Wayne Pate/Illustration Division

Printed in China

CHANTAL AIDA GORDON and **RYAN BENOIT**
are the founders of the award-winning blog *The
Horticult*. Gordon has written for *T: The New York
Times Style Magazine*, *Teen Vogue*, NBC, and
more. As an engineer, photographer, and founder
of Ryan Benoit Design, Benoit invents and designs
modern furniture, fixtures, and planters that have
been featured in the *New York Times*. They live in
Southern California.

thehorticult.com

Clarkson Potter/Publishers
New York
clarksonpotter.com

Also available as an ebook

Cover design by Ian Dingman
Cover photographs by Ryan Benoit